Duty
Discipline
Deposits

By
Jeff Austin, Jr.

*A third generation banker reflects
on how his military service shaped
the man he is today.*

Duty
Discipline
Deposits

Copyright 2025 by Jeff Austin, Jr.

ISBN 09802247-9-9
First Edition, 2025

Published by the SamPat Press
Printed in the United States of America
by Lightning Source, Inc.

Design and layout by Christine Kjosa

Edited by Sam Hopkins

Correspondence and publication requests contact:
SamPat Press
1027 Timothy, Jacksonville, Texas 75766
(903) 586-4488

DEDICATIONS

Dedicated to the memory of my beloved wife,
Sissy Austin

Chapters

Chapter 1   Military Obligation and Decisions

Chapter 2   ROTC-Fort Lee Summer Camp

Chapter 3   Uniforms-Commissioned

Chapter 4   Fort Eustis, VA, - Officers Basic

Chapter 5   Active Duty Assignment

Chapter 6   Extension-Prep for Combat-French Quarter

Chapter 7   Troop Buildup-Training

Chapter 8   STRAC Alert

Chapter 9   Logistical Over the Shore (LOTS Exercise)

Chapter 10   NCO School & President Kennedy

Chapter 11   Lieutenants Protective Association (LPA)

Chapter 12   People and Friends

Chapter 13   Texas Army National Guard

Chapter 14   Take Aways from Army Experience

Duty
Discipline
and Deposits

Chapter 1
Military Obligation and Decisions

The purpose of this autobiographical journal is to preserve my memories of the time served in the U. S. Army and the Texas Army National Guard. I was one of the fortunate few people in uniform whose unit was not involved in actual combat, but was being trained for such action. Bear with me as I fondly remember my military service in the 1960's along with the experiences, the places, mentors and friendships that were made. The gap between 1962, when this was begun and 2025, when it was completed gave me the opportunity to research those years to refresh my memory as well as add a bit of color. I invite you to travel down memory lane with me as I think backward to the 1960's.

This was originally written centered around my writing about my experiences as I was living them (on post and off post). No doubt there will be some embellishments, as time does tend to cloud ones' thoughts. I will try accurately as possible to describe my journey from Frankston High School to ROTC at University of Texas to ROTC Summer camp to Active Duty in the US Army, and finally, the Texas National Guard.

The U.S. Military has changed significantly since this memoir was begun. The draft was eliminated and the country moved to an all-voluntary force, thus a much smaller active-duty military, including all branches. As the numbers declined, more lethal weapons were developed to make up for the reduction of personnel. The various States National Guard units have virtually replaced the Reserve Units of past years in providing infantry, artillery, and armor tactical units. The Guard provides trained personnel to support any war effort.

Chapter 2
Fort Lee Summer Camp

Military service is a period of young men's lives that creates experiences and events that can be found no other place. The experiences and challenges presented during one's period of service vary, but create lasting memories. These memories and experiences are usually preparations for accomplishments in civilian life. As in civilian life, the opportunities are there, but only fate, regulations, discipline, training, opportunities, and determination serve as dominate guidelines in the military as to what is accomplished.

Military service was an obligation cast upon our youthful shoulders after High School graduation in the 1950's. The period of the obligation was six years—only a small price for the freedom we enjoy which was paid for with many lives. One has several doors open through which to enter the military, or to fulfill this obligation. The door I chose to enter bore the name plate – "Reserve Officers Training Corps" when I enrolled at the University of Texas at Austin. The draft and mandatory service was ended in 1973 by President Richard Nixon when the armed forces became an all-volunteer military, but that was after my era of mandatory service.

The University of Texas offered Army, Navy, and Air Force ROTC programs. I chose the Transportation Corps of the Army. The other Army ROTC choices available were Engineer Corps, Military Police and Quartermaster Corps. ROTC was a four-year course of study. We had classroom instruction for two days a week, then one hour of marching drill with M-1 rifles on another day. We had plenty of instruction about the M-1, which was a WWII and Korea weapon. We became proficient for disassembly, reassembly and cleaning of the rifles that were kept in the armory

3

in the basement of Gregory Gymnasium. With the patience of the
ROTC staff and the cadet leaders, we learned to march with the
rifles while learning what is called the Manual of Arms.

The ROTC cadets in the third and fourth year of ROTC were
offered a contract as our commitment to the Army for military
service. A monthly stipend of $91.00 was paid to us, which was
the same compensation that a Private E-1 received monthly when
on active duty. Our ROTC training required our attendance at
a "Summer Camp" between our third and fourth year of study.
Transportation Corp Cadets and Quartermaster Corps from schools
across the nation convened for Summer Camp training in the
summer of 1959 at Fort Lee, Virginia. We were treated as real
recruits during this "Boot Camp" to give us a feel of the real thing.
The summer camp was six weeks of mostly field exercises in
the Virginia summer heat at Fort Lee. Camp A. P. Hill was used
for live fire exercises. Small unit training was all in the field.
Leadership positions were rotated to give cadets exposure to
various levels and types of leadership training. We experienced,
as much as possible, the regular Army routine of early morning
reveille, physical training, formations, classes, and, of course, KP
duty (kitchen police) in garrison and even in the field.

The noise of combat with small arms fire, grenades and other
explosives was a big surprise to me, even if we were using blank
ammunition. This was a good introduction to actual combat and for
the cadets to react. The firing range is always a challenge for safety
and weapon handling. One day we were on the firing line using the
M-1 weapons, when all of a sudden, the order to "cease firing" was
commanded. The instructors became very serious as they moved
us off the firing line because of a safety violation. We learned later
that an intoxicated enlisted person was discovered walking along
the impact area of our weapons at the outer edge of the range. He
was apprehended and a sigh of relief was heard when we learned
that he was not injured, just impaired.

The targets for the Army rifle range were located in bunkers downrange. The known distance firing ranges had firing lines at 100, 300, and 500 meter intervals. We fired M-1 rifles with .30 caliber bullets. There was great communication between the OIC (Officer in Charge) of the firing line and the OIC of the targets at the bunker. The bunker personnel were responsible for raising the targets, scoring the target hits, and repairing the target after each round of firings. The scoring featured a waving red flag if you missed the target and got a zero score for the fired round. The red flag was known as "Maggie's drawers." A bull's eye counted 10 points, and there were scoring rings of 9, 8, and 7. Working in the bunkers was hot, sweaty work. We had to wear our steel helmets in the pits because the bullets bounce around, especially from inexperienced shooters.

Summer camp was not all work. The Camp leaders planned activities on post as well as some leave time to venture off post. The post hosted dances for the cadets. Young ladies from the area were bussed to post to entertain us or dance with us. We enjoyed female company after spending time in the field and being with the troops for 24 hours a day. The festivities were jokingly named "Pig Push" by the cadets. I'm not sure what we were called by the female guests. Actually, they were fun to be with, talk with and entertain, but none of us could leave or make dates with the girls. Just imagine the mixture of local girls with "Horny Cadets." The dances were mandatory, but if nothing was scheduled, we were free to leave post to find recreation. Washington D.C. was a popular destination, as well as other Virginia tourist and historical attractions.

Fort Lee, home of the Quartermaster Corps, is located on the James River. The annual summer camps rotated between Fort Lee and Fort Eustis, which was home of the Transportation Corps. The combat arms (artillery, infantry, engineering, and armor) were held

5

at other bases to accommodate their specialty. The James River Moth Ball Fleet of cargo ships was most evident on the James River. As the name indicates, these ships were in storage and could be activated in a short time to join the fleet.

As we entered other phases of training such as the simulated combat phase, it was a real eye-opener for me. It was a shock to hear the noises of combat. We realized the munitions were blank, but they sounded real. I had no idea how real it would sound. It was shocking, but I soon recovered. It was important to gain confidence with the noise of the munitions. Even though the Transportation Corp is not Infantry by trade, we had to become proficient in Infantry tactics because basically every soldier is Infantry.

I traveled to Fort Lee, Virginia, with classmates George Conn of Beaumont, Texas, and Phil Stotland of Hattiesburg, Mississippi. We met Phil Stotland in Biloxi, Mississippi, at a club along US 90. Phil was a regular at this club, which offered liquor, gambling and betting, which were all illegal in Mississippi at the time. The return home was a bit slower than the trip to Fort Lee, but we did enjoy sites and attractions, and we had been paid for our time. Our return trip included a stop at the R.J. Reynolds Tobacco Company in Winston-Salem, NC, where we watched the manufacturing of cigarettes. Later we listened to George Conn play his newly acquired pawn shop guitar.

The ROTC summer camp experience provided a basis for selecting Cadet Officers during our senior year of college. I was a Company Commander for the 1959 fall semester and on the Battalion Staff as a Major during the spring of 1960 semester. The senior year of ROTC honed the skills learned at summer camp, for example: map reading, leadership, weapon handling and the development of military bearing that would be valuable in Active duty.

The Army, Navy and Air Force ROTC programs at UT rotated the responsibility of flag duty at the Main Building. The American and State of Texas flags were raised and lowered each day, and the ROTC units provided the personnel to perform the duty. As a freshman I was on this detail and impressed by the process. The details formed up, one for the Texas flag and the other for the American flag. The American flag is the first to be raised and the last to be lowered. We had to learn precise marching and handling of the flags including proper folding of them. Just being on campus early mornings for raising our flags was an emotional experience for me. This was just a little part of daily campus life. Everyone noticed the flags, but probably did not realize that student ROTC members performed this important duty.

U. of Texas ROTC
Cadet Jeff Austin, Jr.

7

ROTC Summer Camp Cadet Unit

**At ROTC Summer camp the Army PT
Exam had overhead climbing bars**

**Cadet Austin was in ROTC Summer Camp
Company B**

**ROTC Cadets Passing in Review During a
Summer Camp Parade**

Chapter 3
Uniforms and Graduation

Commissioning Exercises served as my graduation day from the University of Texas in August 1960. The military custom is for the sergeants to line up to render the first salute to the newly commissioned officers. There was a line seeking to give the first salute in order to be paid a dollar by the lieutenant to the first person who saluted him.

Uniforms!!! A must in the military. Each newly commissioned officer receives a uniform allowance. Let's just agree that it was $400.00, for that figure sounds about right for uniform purchases in 1960. Sol Frank & Company of San Antonio was in 1960 a renowned uniform provider for America's military. The Class A uniforms for the Army officers changed during our ROTC years from the brown shoe, brown jacket and tan pants uniform to the black shoe, green jacket and pants uniform. Still authorized were the TW's tan uniform jacket and pants, as were khaki pants with long and short sleeve khaki shirts. The work uniform called fatigues were solid green. Oh, don't forget the formal Dress Blue Uniform, which consisted of a dark blue jacket, lighter blue pants with a gold stripe down the pant legs, with matching hat.

So, a trip to San Antonio was necessary to be measured and fitted for active-duty uniforms. I was so excited that I spent almost all of the allowance purchasing the green Class A uniform and the TW Class A tan uniform. Very little was left over for fatigues and khakis I had to buy on active duty from the commissary. I did purchase a formal uniform from my friend and fraternity brother Doyle Perkinson. Very little alterations were needed. I probably wore this uniform five times during active duty. After active duty, I was able to sell the formal and dress green uniform to friends entering the Army.

I received a commission as a Second Lieutenant in the Army of The United States upon graduation from UT on 17 August 1960. At that time, I had orders to report for six months active duty in March 1961. The decision to serve six months active duty and the balance of my obligation in the active reserve was based on my employment commitment to First National Bank of Jacksonville. I wanted to fulfill my military obligation and return to Jacksonville. Most of my University of Texas classmates decided to volunteer for six months active duty. Little did we know that in a few months' time of being on active duty, we would be extended on active duty for a year.

Newly commissioned 2LT Jeff Austin, Jr., in cotton khaki uniform

11

**LT Austin enjoyed eating beignets at the
Café du Monde in the French Quarter**

Shining boots on active duty

Chapter 4
Fort Eustis, VA, Officers Basic Class

I boarded the Missouri Pacific Eagle in Jacksonville for a train ride to Fort Eustis, Virginia. Just as I was about to step into the Pullman car, I was handcuffed by Jacksonville Chief of Police Archie Cook and Special Texas Ranger Jimmy Staton. They escorted me to my seat in cuffs in a most lawman professional manner. I was very surprised and thought there was a reason for the cuffs. A criminal offense would end my military career before it started. They began to laugh, and then I understood this was just a prank. The other passengers enjoyed the arrest also. My friends from UT bound for Fort Eustis wondered what happened to me in Jacksonville that would warrant being cuffed and led on the train. We all had a great chuckle and moved on for further Army training.

Fort Eustis, Virginia, is south of Richmond and is located in the section of Virginia known as the Peninsula. This base, once a game preserve, is the home of the Army Transportation Corps which would be our "home" for about nine weeks as we completed the Basic Officers Orientation Course. Located within 60 miles of the base were several important military installations such as: Langley Field, Norfolk Naval Station, Portsmouth Naval Base, Little Creek Marine Base, to mention a few. The Orientation Course is one of hundreds of courses on transportation offered through the Transportation School at Fort Eustis. It is here that concepts of transportation are developed to meet the needs of the modern, mobile, mechanized Army.

As students, we were subjected to a few minor harassments to "Shape Up." General military subjects were first on the schedules to introduce us to other branches of the Army. We migrated from classroom to the field training phase of our course for approximately three weeks. During this period, we lived

13

in temporary barracks, converted to BOQ's (Bachelor Officers Quarters) which provided each officer with a cubicle of his own. We had daily inspections of equipment, plus inspections on the weekends.

I received a real jolt from one of our training officers during an inspection. I could not recite the accurate serial number of my issued weapon. My actions were unforgiveable, for all soldiers are expected to know that number. The captain threatened that I could be downgraded and lose my commission. Never again did I forget that serial number. (During that inspection, I made up a number, and that did not go over well, thus the threats.) The field training phase was designed to give us an experience of infantry tactics. We also were exposed to the mission of the Transportation Corps of moving people and material to support troops in battle situations. We were exposed to loading and unloading trains, aircraft, boats, and trucks, as well as maintaining scheduling the modes of transportation.

Completion of the 9-week orientation course meant we were qualified to assume roles of platoon leaders in units throughout the Army. Our orders were received a week before graduation, assigning us to various commands. As was the custom then, most RFA (Reserve Force Army) Officers were reassigned to an installation, preferably a Transportation Corps Base, near their home of record or to an installation in their home Army area. I was assigned to the Transportation Terminal Command, Gulf, located in New Orleans, Louisiana. Placed on the same orders with me were five other officers from Texas, Arkansas, Alabama, and Louisiana.

There was some free time during the Orientation course when we were allowed weekend passes. One specific weekend, I visited my friend James I. Perkins from Rusk, Texas. Jim and I met during our Boy Scout days attending the Jamboree at Valley Forge, PA in 1950, as well as in Methodist Youth Fellowship meetings, and high school athletics. Jim preceded me at UT and the Phi Delta Theta fraternity.

Jim was a Navy Ensign stationed on the USS Valley Forge, which was a small aircraft carrier refitted to carry helicopters. Somehow, I found transportation to visit Jim. He probably drove to Fort Eustis, for he had his car, and I did not. I was impressed by the carrier and the activity around its berth at the Norfolk Naval Station. Army 2nd Lieutenant Austin, and Ensign Perkins dined in the Officers Mess on the ship. I was most impressed at the service, menu and high-ranking officers dining with us. Just imagine being in the training phase of the Army, then visiting a real ship of the fleet whose mission is to fight the enemy. We were able to use our rank as 2LT to visit the Officer Clubs at other military installations in the area. We even visited Fort Monroe, Virginia, which was headquarters of the Continental Army Command. Many high-ranking officers were there also, but we were well received and served with tolerance.

Life-long friendships were begun at Fort Eustis among the young officers. Specifically, they were Betty and Jay Cummins who lived off post in the area. I think Betty was the only wife to accompany their officer to Fort Eustis in our class. They were longtime sweethearts from

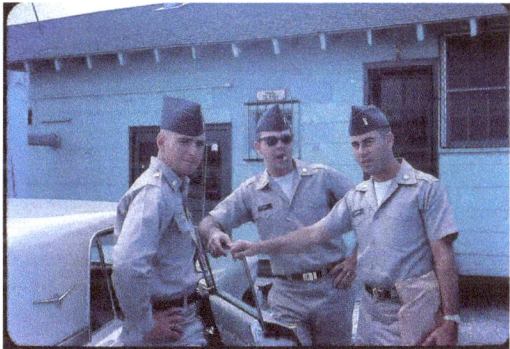

Three amigos – Lt. Jeff Austin, Lt. Jim Cox, Lt. Jay Cummins

Monroe, Louisiana. They were kind enough to give me a ride to Shreveport, LA, when we completed the Officers Basic Course. We alternated drivers and drove straight to Monroe, LA, their home.

Chapter 5
Assignment to Active Duty

Transportation Terminal Command, Gulf (TTCG) was organized under the Terminal Concept of the Transportation Corps, which organized similar commands on the Atlantic Coast and on the Pacific Coast. The terminal at New Orleans is located on Dauphine Street at the intersection of the Industrial Canal and the Mississippi River. Camp Leroy Johnson (CLJ), a subordinate command of TTCG, is located on Lake Pontchartrain some seven miles from the terminal. CLJ supports the TTCG by providing housing facilities and training for assigned personnel.

Camp Leroy Johnson was opened in 1942 as the New Orleans Army Air Base. In 1947, the base was renamed after World War II Medal of Honor recipient Leroy Johnson. Johnson was a native of Caney Creek near Oakdale, Louisiana, and served as a Sergeant, U S Army. He died near Leyte, Philippine Islands, shortly after he threw himself on two unexploded Japanese grenades during an assault, thus saving two comrades. After WWII, Camp Leroy Johnson became a permanent transportation training center, as well as a replacement center and a training center for Army Reserve units. The post was officially closed by the Department of Defense on June 30, 1964.

After a 15-day leave, the journey was made to New Orleans to report for duty and find housing. A French Quarter apartment in the 800 block of Bourbon Street, in the neighborhood of Pete Fountain's club as well as Al Hirt's club, was occupied until August 18, 1961. After I was extended on active duty, I moved to the Caton Court in the Gentilly section of New Orleans, near Lake Pontchartrain.

I was assigned to the 394th Transportation Battalion (Terminal Service) on June 15, 1961, and further assigned to the 569th Transportation Company. There I received my first taste of Army Life-Camp Leroy Johnson style. My duties were varied, but the principal duty initially was as a Platoon Leader. Eventually, as our unit decreased in size, I became the unit Executive Officer, merely because there were only two Officers: Captain Edward Dardis and myself.

The first task assigned to me was the support of a Reserve Company from Gulfport, Mississippi, which was at CLJ for two weeks of active duty. Upon completion of these two weeks, I bid farewell to Captain Shields of that Company and told him I was a short timer and would be out of the Army in September. Little did I know that I would be the first person he saw when his unit returned for active duty in October 1961. An assignment to a small unit like the 569th gave me an opportunity to learn how the Army functions and to become familiar with the organization of a Terminal Service Company. I was able to learn about the administration of the unit, thus gaining firsthand knowledge of the eternal "Red Tape." I learned the importance of the First Sergeant, for that person actually ran the company.

At CLJ, Department of Army civilian advisors were evident, and they were at our transportation port. These highly classified civilians were probably retired soldiers with outstanding records. They had no command authority or responsibilities, but advised the unit commanders on training matters, health issues, policies, and many more matters. I was not sure if there was an approved ratio of civilian advisers to the number of active duty units or the number of commanders.

The Terminal Service Company is perhaps the largest TOE (Table Organization Equipment) in the Army. It is designed to

17

work one ship, both on board and on the shore continually on a 24-hour basis. The unit has two Ship Platoons and two Shore Platoons, which work according to their name designation. The Shore Platoon has most of the equipment, which includes trucks, forklifts, cranes, bulldozers, duplication equipment and lighting units. It is impressive to see all this equipment operating on shore moving cargo to the supply depot. On the other hand, it is also depressing to see the equipment sit idle for many months and watch the battle between man and nature. The battle is to combat rust, mildew, and other destructive agents that pop up when machinery is idle in a damp climate.

Young Officers like me had many learning experiences, and one time or the other had several additional titles with responsibility like Pay Officer, Training Officer, Legal Affairs Officer, CBR (Chemical Biological Radiological) Officer, Insurance Officer, and the list goes on. I never shall forget my inexperience while participating in a Court Martial. I was the trial counsel, or prosecutor, and was really embarrassed, for I was not prepared. I also served as a defense counsel and did better.

We learned to make lesson plans for classroom instruction on various subjects. We had the opportunity to learn about many different military subjects as we taught the classes. We probably bored the soldiers, but the class had to go on. Films were a favorite of the instructors since we did not have to instruct as much.

As a Pay Officer, my duty was to pay members of our company. In 1961-1962, the troops were paid once a month and in cash. As I remember, payday was the last working day of the month and was considered to be a holiday. In 1961-62, the Private E-1 pay was $91.00 per month, but if he was married there was an allowance for the spouse. A 2LT pay was $222.30 month. The Pay Officer rode to 7500 (the port) to pick up the money and vouchers to pay our company. I was accompanied by a driver and a guard. Upon returning to the company headquarters, money would be attached to the vouchers to wait for troops to arrive from the Payday parade.

We had to be careful with the cash, for the Finance Division had given us the correct amount of cash broken down to the correct bills to use. Once all balanced, the individuals began receiving their pay. They would walk up salute, give their name, verify the receipt of cash, then salute, then about face and march out. There was usually poker, crap games and other games of chance in the barracks. Of course, there were losers and winners. If pay was lost, the enlisted personnel could eat free of charge at the Mess Hall, have free laundry, and free uniform replacement, if needed.

CLJ operated 24 hours a day, so someone had to be at Headquarters after normal work hours. This assignment was from 1800 hours to 0600, or from reveille to taps, as the Duty Officer or maybe the Officer of the Day (OD). The duties included a tour of the base and its training areas to inspect the guards, tour the Mess Halls, Infirmary, and Motor Pool. The duty station of the Officer of the Day was CLJ headquarters, and we had to be available to answer calls from higher commands, especially if an alert or emergency presented itself.

We were assigned to the OD room in the Officers Bachelor Quarters. A driver was assigned for the tours of the facility. We were on duty for the What Ifs, etc. During one of my tours as OD, I visited our remote training area on the Industrial Canal. Swampy Louisiana land surrounded the training area. Coffee and conversation were good with the non-commissioned officers (NCOs) on watch there. On one occurrence I remember being told about the Northern troops trying to pet a nutria (swamp rat with sharp teeth). This trooper ended up with a severe bite, while the nutria retreated safely to the swamp.

The organizations stationed at Camp Leroy Johnson participated not only with training reserve units, but especially with General Shep Morrison's division. Morrison was a former Mayor of New Orleans and annually led his division to Grand Isle, Louisiana for training. Another mission of the Camp Leroy Johnson units was the annual re-supply of U.S. military installations in Greenland and Iceland. Detachments from CLJ would journey to Thule, Greenland to assist in movement of equipment and material to the bases during their "summer". The guys who participated in these assignments enjoyed the mission and challenge. These missions were resumed after the Berlin Crisis passed; therefore, I never had to be detached to Iceland or Greenland.

A typical day for troops stationed at Camp Leroy Johnson began early with reveille, with an order to fall in, which means the troops line up accordingly with their squads and platoon, in order to be counted. The purpose of this early formation is to determine that all are present that should be present. The First Sergeant takes the report and passes the information to the Reveille Officer. After reveille, the troops have breakfast in the Mess Hall and then report in formation for the daily physical training (PT) prior to attending the training scheduled for the day.

Being the Reveille Officer means you have to report to post earlier than usual. When I was living in the French Quarter, I was dressed in the uniform of the day and received odd stares from the party-people just retiring for the night. I would really get the looks when I purchased coffee and beignets at the Morning Call restaurant in the French Quarter. This Reveille duty was rotated among the junior officers, as was leading the PT for the Battalion.

The first alert, when all troops were ordered back to post, was the alert for Hurricane Carla. The base was on high alert for whatever might happen if the storm hit New Orleans or our services were needed elsewhere. New Orleans escaped the wrath of Carla which hit Galveston, Texas City, and that part of the Texas Gulf Coast. The officers spent most of the alert in the Officer's Club preparing for action.

We truly did see some action, for our DUKW Company was ordered to proceed to Galveston and Texas City where the DUKWS were vital in the flooded area. The DUKW, commonly known as the "Duck", is a six-wheeled amphibious vehicle used extensively by the U.S. military during World War II for transporting troops and supplies over land and water. The name DUKW is derived from the GMC model nomenclature: "D" for the year 1942, "U" for utility (amphibious), "K" for all-wheel drive, and "W" for dual rear axles. I really tried to volunteer for the trip, but was unable to convince higher grade Officers that I needed to go.

The BARC (Barge, Amphibious, Resupply, Cargo) could be considered to be a DUKW on steroids. The Army had very few BARC's whose mission was to load material offshore and bring it to the depot. It had much greater capacity than a DUKW. I had last seen one while at Virginia Beach during my Officers Basic Class, which was a short-lived experience it seems.

The 569 Transportation Company Barracks

The Famous BARC Amphibious Vehicle
for Carrying Cargo

Army Armored Personnel Carrier (APC)

Training on unloading cargo to BARC's

Troops passing in review on Pay Day

LT's in their Jeep

Chapter 6
Extension- Prep for Deployment
French Quarter

The summer of 1961 was filled with routine Army details until the middle of August when black clouds of possible war began to gather over Western Europe, mostly over Berlin. These clouds were seen everywhere politicians gathered. However, the Commander-in-Chief (President John F. Kennedy) thought the world situation grave enough to activate 150,000 National Guard and Reserve personnel. Personnel on active duty were "frozen" on duty as many received extensions of service for 12 months. I was one of those soldiers who got extended. Our orders dated September 5, 1961, informed us that we had an additional 12 months of active-duty service according to the President of the United States "without our permission." During my extension, the Cold War got hotter. In October 1962, the Cuban Missile Crisis occurred. The Russians began to build missile sites in Cuba that could launch nuclear weapons against the USA. President John F. Kennedy blockaded Cuba so Russia could not smuggle atomic bombs into that country. This was the closest America ever came to a much feared atomic World War III. Naturally, we wondered what would happen to us.

During this period of buildup, all personnel began to work together preparing for possible moveouts. Our STRAC units (Strategic Army Corps), or (Skilled, Tough, Ready Around the Clock) units were alerted for possible movement to Europe during the fall. I was transferred to the 71st Transportation Company, where I assumed the primary duty as the Shore Platoon Leader. The Special Order 178 was effective October 4, 1961, with a MOS of 0804.

Prior to my extension and transfer it was my task to inform members of the 569th Company that certain units in the Battalion were alerted.

25

The men were warned they could be moved to strategic units if needed and were warned to observe security practices. However, the men to whom I addressed remained with the 569th and I was the one who was transferred to a strategic unit, the 71st Transportation Company, commanded by Captain Rust.

After I learned about the one-year extension on my active duty time, there was the need to find different housing. An unfurnished apartment was located in the Gentilly section of New Orleans. There was no encouragement from superior officers on whether or not our units would be moving out, but a lease was signed. The apartment was on Caton Court. Other officers living in the area were Jay Cummins, Jim Cox, and Stuart Chancellor.

Moving from the French Quarter with all its activity to a quieter neighborhood was quite a change. The hustle, bustle, and lively French Quarter was a great place to live at that time. As you walked the streets, you recognized other Quarter citizens and felt as if we were one large apartment complex. We were able to park on the streets and know the "barkers" outside the clubs. My Bourbon Street apartment was a few doors from Pete Fountain's club, as well as Al Hirt, the trumpet player's club. These entertainers were well known.

The strip joints had real girls for strippers, and did they have talent. One had marching breasts; another could twirl small propellers with hers. The Queen of the strip clubs was Chris Owens who enjoyed 66 years of entertainment in the Quarter. Dancing in form fitting, glittering outfits of her own design, her showmanship was classic with plunging necklines and high hemlines dancing in high heels with athletic dance steps. Yes, club "809" was a classy strip joint which opened in 1956. (for more info on Chris, Google " Chris Owens").

Tom Fitzgerald, formerly of Frankston, Texas, operated Kelly's Bar across Canal Street from the Roosevelt Hotel. Uncle Tom, as I knew him in Frankston, had operated bars in New Orleans for years. His wife, Aunt Fred, had relatives in Frankston, but after tiring of the bar scene they moved to Frankston in late 1940s. He ran the Frankston Crate Factory which produced wooden crates, baskets, and tomato lugs for the marketing of produce grown in the Frankston area. He probably returned to New Orleans part time, then full time in the late 1950s. I always enjoyed visits to Kelly's to learn more about New Orleans (I paid for my drinks). Tom would recommend restaurants, as well as clubs to visit.

During the Mardi Gras season, I visited Kelly's and noticed some unusual changes, the front window and front entry door were removed. The tables and chairs were also stacked leaving a lot of open space. Tom's explanation was very simple: Many patrons of the bar, during the Mardi Gras parades and celebrations, had no place to stay and tried to sleep in the bar. With the tables and chairs stacked, they had no luck at Kelly's. The open front window allowed the waiters to serve patrons without entering the building.

Speaking of Mardi Gras, I did attend the BIG parade on Fat Tuesday, and was it ever an experience for a Frankston, Texas boy. Just use your imagination for the costumes, clothes, no clothes, alcohol, bands, noise, and noise makers; just people having a great time. Yes, it was fun, interesting living in the French Quarter, but reality had to take over, to seek less-expensive quarters.

I cannot leave this section without mentioning the star attractions at Pat O'Brien's (other than the Hurricane drinks). Before Cher, Madonna and Beyonce, there was MERCEDES, who was the star of the "Dueling Pianos". She was joined on stage by Connie Kay, and Sara Belle "Sue Wheeler". They were the pioneers and made it look easy. They could

27

play any tune and played to the audience who also sang along. Mercedes performed at Pat O'Brien's for 32 years and is still a legend. The piano players incorporated modern music, audience interaction, college fight song battles, and song requests.

Not to be forgotten or overlooked is the Legend Eddie "The Rhythm Man" Gabriel. Mr. Eddie was a fixture at O'Brien's for nearly 67 years. Eddie would stroll to the stage and begin playing the "metal pans or trays". With thimbles on his fingers, he would beat out rhythms on the bottom of the pans. Eddie and the piano players would play off one another. The audience would toss coins at the pans, and Eddie was quite adept at catching them. Mercedes, Mr. Eddie, Connie Kay, and "Sue", along with cheerful crowds drinking Hurricanes, were the Pat O'Brien's of my time in New Orleans. This was truly unforgettable entertainment and safe fun times.

St. Louis Cathedral, and its square area facing the Mississippi River was a great place to just people watch. Artists set up around the square, horse carriage rides were available, as were street musicians. Just sitting with a beverage created great memories. Shops and restaurants surrounded the area. The Pontalba Buildings form two sides of Jackson Square in the French Quarter. These matching red-brick, one-block-long, four story buildings were built between 1849-1851. The ground floors housed shops and restaurants. The upper floors are apartments, which, reputedly are the oldest continuously rented such apartments in the United States.

The Cabildo, an elegant building, neighbors the St. Louis Cathedral on another side of the Square. This building was the site of the Louisiana Purchase transfer ceremonies in 1803. The Cabildo was in charge of all ordinary aspects of municipal government - policing, sanitation, taxation, the supervision of building, price and wage regulation, and the administration of justice. The Cabildo is also a Louisiana State Museum and houses many rare artifacts of American History. It was originally called the "Casa Capitular" and was the seat of Spanish colonial City Hall. The history, artists, music, restaurants, and movement of people makes the Jackson Square area very popular with citizens and visitors.

I had the good fortune to have visitors during my time in the French Quarter, not only from family, but from friends. Aunt Helen Austin and son John F. Austin, III (Johnny), along with young John's girlfriend at the time, were also visitors. We were treated to Brennan's and Pascal's Manale. Pascal's Manale's claim to fame was the creation of New Orleans barbeque shrimp. What a treat to eat and enjoy these shrimp, but it was messy, which made it all the better.

During the visit to Manale's, we were introduced to a local architect, Collin Diboll. His office was in the "Other Alley", not the Pirates Alley, which was the famous alley next to the St. Louis Cathedral. Diboll and friends were not very busy during the depression and prohibition, so they created a chart that would provide a guide for proper mixing of cocktails. The chart not only had recipes for the drinks, but the type of glass to use, the best time of day for certain drinks, along with some toasts. An example of toasts: "Some are fond of drinking and others of high positions, but we're for toleration and down with prohibition." This chart is truly a New Orleans treasure as it includes sketches of famous historic landmarks, as well as sketches of dining, dancing, entertainment, sporting events, and carriage rides. I was fortunate enough to obtain a copy, and have it framed over our bar at our home in Jacksonville, Texas.

Uncle John and friend Jack Perry had real estate interests in and around New Orleans. Their local contact person was Ed Hamilton who was quite an operator. He was the person who wanted the photos of President Kennedy to present to the Mayor of the City, Victor Schiro. I assume Hamilton was the person that persuaded John Austin and

Jack Perry to buy the Solaris Drug and Fine Food located on Royal Street across from the Monteleone Hotel. The name was used to open a restaurant in Houston, which had a good reputation but a brief life.

My parents visited and were talked into bringing my boat to New Orleans. I'm not sure that Jeff Sr. had much, if any, experience pulling a boat. They arrived safely with the boat in good condition. This was truly an act of love to bring this Glastron boat with a 50 hp motor to me, and it was appreciated. The motor had been maintained before the trip, but not good enough. The first time boating in Lake Pontchartrain we had motor failure and had to be towed in. Talk about embarrassment with my Army friends. However, we made several more water ski trips without any problems. We all observed that the lake was not pristine, so we began crossing the causeway to the Tchefuncte River for much better water.

Three Navy cadets stationed in Meridian, MS, visited and took in the nightlife. The Ensigns were Roy D. (Butch) Shank, Don Haberle, and Paul Davis. Paul was the only one to complete flight school and become a Navy aviator. He later flew United Airlines. Don Haberle was stationed at a Navy Depot in Memphis, TN, while Butch served as Supply Officer on a ship.

Hanging around in the French Quarter

Brenda and Charlie Martin

My boat used for water skiing on Lake Pontchartrain

My ski buddies out on the water

Charlie Martin upright on his skis

Chapter 7
Troop Build Up and Training

The buildup of troops caused a lot of activity at Camp Leroy Johnson. An Army Reserve Transportation Battalion from Brooklyn, New York, was activated making CLJ home to two Transportation Battalions. The Units of the 394th were built up to full strategic strength. We received a great number of recruits in October and November. To fully train these men, we had to initiate training programs to supplement their basic training. In addition to training ourselves, we were given the assignment of instructing and supporting the newly activated reserve companies. Many long hours were logged by key NCOs and officers of our Company. For once, everybody had a goal: "Get Ready to Move."

The 49th Armored Division of the Texas Army National Guard was activated during this period of 1961 and reopened at Fort Polk in Leesville, Louisiana. The Jacksonville, Texas outfit was among the activated units. Indeed, the Berlin Crisis was taken seriously by the TTCG. Activity increased throughout the command as evidenced by an increase in exports of military equipment and supplies during the second quarter of FY 1962. The buildup moves ordered by our President was questioned by many people, both military and civilians. However, I believe the buildup of personnel and materials was successful in blocking a shooting war for the time being.

Tension was at its height, when seven Officers from our Command were hastily ordered to Europe. One Officer was our Company Commander, Captain Rust of the 71st. This was a classified mission, but his parting words were to the effect that he would be looking for us in Europe. This statement was supported by an innocent looking envelope

33

received through Distribution. Inside the packet which came from the CONARC (Continental Army Command) in Fort Monroe, VA, was the literature for units preparing to journey to Europe. Road signs in French were posted in various buildings as a result; then tension certainly was mounting.

We received a new Commanding Officer for the 71st, a First Lieutenant from our sister unit, but a rival company. LT Lawrence Franks had just returned from an exercise, was extended indefinitely, and given a command, all at the same time. At one time we had nine 2nd Lieutenants in the 71st. We all admitted inexperience, but we did our best to overcome that obstacle. Eventually, the officers were shifted around the Battalion, but for a while we were running and tripping over each other. Actually, my replacement was on base, as well as my replacement's replacement.

Another proof of the serious buildup was the arrival of the SS Ancon as a training aid for both of the Terminal Service Battalions. Our training area was on the Industrial Canal, which connected Lake Pontchartrain and the Mississippi River. This once proud ship was a relic from WWII, had been used by the Panama Canal Company, and now was to be used by soldiers. The old ship did not know what the future held, but the troopers seemed to enjoy working cargo on her. This additional training aid made it possible to train 16 hours daily or to train two shifts daily that included the Ship and Shore platoons from companies stationed at CLJ. Our readiness date arrived and departed with no definite change. What happened around the policy table and classified conferences, I do not know; however, we were not moved. Tension began to ease after Christmas 1961.

A Navel Craft Used for Training Ship to Shore Exercises

Front Loader Equipment Exhibit Ready for Inspection

Chapter 8
STRAC Alerts - Continued Training

When the threat of buildup had been exhausted, the officers had to turn to other means to provide incentives to train our Company. Our most useful weapon was the STRAC ALERT or Mobility Test; but running a close second was the I.G. (Inspector General) inspection, then just plain inspections.

Inspection of the soldiers in the barracks was regular and announced. The platoon leaders led the inspection of their platoon. Each soldier had a foot locker which contained underwear, socks, a razor, toothbrush, and other personal grooming items. The razor was expected to be clean. We soon learned that each person had an inspection razor and a daily use razor which was not on exhibit. As I was in front of one soldier, I asked where the shaving cream was. He replied he did not use shaving cream, but used Nair instead. This caused some snicker and laughter from the inspecting party, for Nair is a cream that would remove facial hair without the use of a razor. This leaves a very clean razor for inspection.

The use of Nair was not the only unusual event of barrack inspection. Word came to the officers that a gun was found in the foot locker of a soldier who was being intensely questioned about the matter. He was stammering and trying to explain. When I saw the pistol, I instantly recognized it as a Circle N toy pistol made by the Nichols Industries of Jacksonville, Texas. I'm sure I saved the soldier some disciplinary action by knowing that it was a toy. Everyone relaxed and life went on.

One part of the barracks that we did not inspect was the section occupied by the cooks. Each company had a field kitchen and cooks to use it. When in garrison, the company cooks worked shifts at the Mess Hall. So due to their shift work, we did not mess with the cooks. K.P.

36

duty was performed by personnel assigned by the First Sergeant of each company, which freed the cooks to only cook. The Army had a master menu for the entire Army and supplied the food for preparation. The local cooks had the latitude to improvise the recipes and use their talents to make the food tasty for the troops. Actually, we had some great cooks that performed masterfully when we were in the field.

The new year 1962 brought a big freeze, which hit us hard. Not expecting such severe weather, we tended to overlook antifreeze liquid in some of our vehicles. Much to our despair and uncomfortable thoughts, we had several casualties including cracked motor blocks and frozen radiators among our equipment. Many extra hours of vigil against the freezing weather were experienced by motor pool men, as well as by the officers. The final accounting revealed only two severely damaged fork-lifts out of 16. Not really good, but some hell was raised over the damage anyway.

All was calm around CLJ until the last week in February when the long-expected Mobility Test was initiated. It was a requirement for STRAC Units of our classification to be able to move from the home station with full TOE (men and equipment) within 72 hours. This test is designed to check the efficiency of a unit, the accuracy of the SOP (Standard Operating Procedures) and the ability of key men, both Officers and NCOs.

The alert was called on a Tuesday morning by a team of officers from the Fourth Army Headquarters. From that moment until the termination of the exercise, these Officers were to be observing all our actions from assembly to load out. I happened to be at Camp Villere in Slidell, Louisiana, when the alert was issued, therefore, I along with three other officers, had to hurry back to CLJ in order to participate in the exercise.

Camp Villere was a World War II Camp established in 1942 in Tammany Parish near Slidell, Louisiana. The camp was named after Jacques Philippe Villere, a Louisiana State Militia major general during the War of 1812 and the state's second governor. The camp had a small arms range for the trainees of the Army in the New Orleans area as well as for the Louisiana National Guard. In the 1960s it was converted into a tactical training center for the troops at Camp Leroy Johnson. The 1710 acre camp area contained barracks, mess hall, gun ranges, and airfield. As of 2025, Camp Villere is an active Louisiana National Guard post with approximately 1,850 acres. Approximately 1,500 acres are protected and preserved through an agreement with the Nature Conservancy.

There were many requirements and tests to determine our readiness during the STRAC Test. The experienced leadership in our battalion and especially our company, the 71st Transportation Company led by 1LT Larry Franks, provided the knowledge for us to be successful. LT. Franks supervised the making of a chart which scheduled events in order of completion. Among those events were: technical inspections of all equipment, personnel shakedowns, preparation of personal affairs kits, inoculations, and packing the CONEX boxes. Needless to say, some of us remained awake for several consecutive hours. We passed the test with flying colors and were ready to move out within some 60 hours.

The inspection team consisted of knowledgeable Officers and Non-Coms from the Fourth Army headquarters in San Antonio, TX, as well as the Continental Army Command at Fort Monroe, Virginia. The team was large enough that several were assigned to each unit. To keep busy the days and weeks after the alert, I had a few extra details to perform. The one I enjoyed was the role of Umpire and Aggressor leader in war games staged with the Brooklyn Battalion of reserves at Camp Villere, Louisiana. Other Officers on this detail were: 1LT Bob Crowe, Larry Marselik, and Greg Eucyer. Our job was to umpire and be the harassing aggressors and then attack the participating units. We would attack the road march of friendly troops and then harass them during the hours of darkness to test their perimeter defense. This was serious training that was much needed, but we had fun and tried to be creative.

Training to Offload Cargo

Chapter 9 LOGISTICAL OVER THE SHORE *(LOTS Exercise)*

Now that the Berlin Crisis has passed, and we were not being shipped out, it was back to regular training. Two Terminal Battalions were in CLJ that needed more training. I had been transferred from the 71st Transportation Company to the Headquarters of the 394th BN as an Assistant S-3 (operations officer) serving with Major Edward Dardis, my former CO while in the 569th Company, along with 1st Lt Robert (Bob) Crowe. My MOS (Military Occupational Specialty) was 2162.

Our Battalion, the 394th Transportation Battalion (terminal), participated in the LOTS Exercise (Logical Over the Shore). The purpose of this exercise was: 1) Conduct the Army Training Test; 2) Familiarization Firing of crew-served weapons; 3) Specialized tactical and logistical training of all units; and 4) a visitors' day. Movement from CLJ to Port St. Joe, Florida, began on March 26, 1962, with the advance parties consisting of elements of the 394th Battalion units. They arrived at the training site on March 27 and until April 2 were engaged in clearing and grading a pre-selected administrative bivouac site for the remaining of the companies of the battalion. The main body of the convoy departed Camp Leroy Johnson to arrive at Port St. Joe on April 2, 1962. We camped overnight while enroute at Eglin Field in Florida, which trained the pilots of General Doolittle's command prior to the WWII raid on Japan and was used for Green Beret training for several years.

All units of the 394th made the trip along US Hwy 90 before it became I-10. Units included the 458 T Company (DUKW), Boat Company (562nd) with 6 LCM-8s, 2 BTs, 2 BARCs, a Q-boat, one LT and one ST (all various sizes of Landing Craft).

As Assistant S-3, I worked with LT Crowe and Major Dardis to assist the communitarians in setting up lines for communications, organizing and supervising training.

We were actually on the St. Joe Spit. The prevailing winds brought over the paper mill smell from the mainland every night. (Just remember the smell of the paper mills in Lufkin, Texas.) The terminal service companies were able to perform their assigned mission under realistic conditions. Changing surf conditions presented hazards that were easily overcome by personnel on the ships, personnel driving the DUKW's and by unit equipment. The LCM's watercraft were our transportation to the mainland to St. Joe and Panama City. Several of the Lieutenants commandeered jeeps and drivers for the weekends so we were able to get off the Spit. We were wearing Class A khakis and life jackets, ready for fun.

Tactical training was an integral part of the LOTS exercise. Numerous situations were developed, such as CBR attacks, guerrilla activities, air attacks, firefighting, and rear area defense, to test the versatility of each individual unit. The S-3 section senior officers, Major Dardis, and LT. Crowe, were ruled out of the game, thus leaving one 2/LT Austin to be the Operations officer for the Battalion during these "attacks." They tell me, and I remember, that I performed well. (I would not write otherwise.)

Lifestyle on the Spit? Really not too bad, days were rather warm, nights a bit cooler, but Army life settled into a routine. Reveille, work details, and classes taught on various subjects were the coordinated purpose of the LOTS. Taps came after work, before sundown, leaving free time for showers.

The cook sections of the organizations were set up, with each company hosting some of the headquarters' staff and support troops. The cooks were free to use their imagination in food preparation which pleased all. We must have set up a commissary for we had beer (or at least the officers did), and the availability of personal items for sale. A laundry was set up, as was a barber chair, as well as mail service. Life was as good as it could be on a sandy piece of land surrounded by the Gulf of Mexico, using shower tents, latrines, battling the wind, chiggers, and the paper mill smell. We knew civilization was near by observing the coastal city lights.

The LOTS ended with a visitors' day. There were two Brigadier Generals plus a host of local dignitaries from Panama City, St. Joe, and surrounding cities. They all enjoyed viewing the BARQ's, DUKW's, forklifts, and men simulating real conditions. I escorted Brigadier General Losey.

It was time to return to CLJ. I was the officer in charge of the Advance Road guards. Our mission was to place a soldier-guard at vital road intersections to keep the troop convoy on the right road. We left the Spit early, early in the morning. About mid-morning, we were probably in Eastern Mississippi after transversing the Florida panhandle and a quick zip through lower Alabama. As we entered Mississippi, it was time to have a break and grab a bite to eat.

We stopped at a roadside cafe, and entered through the front door, and were quickly told that the African-American guys had to enter and eat through the rear door. That comment did not set well with me. We were all in the uniform of the U.S. Army, but that did not matter. I told the guys to get back in the truck and we would find another spot. They said it was ok to go the rear, but we did get in the truck and find another cafe down the road. It was just not right to treat our troops like that regardless of race, color, or creed. We did arrive safely back in NOLA.

Aerial view of camp site at the St. Joe Spit

LT Martin leading training class at St. Joe Spit

Practicing unloading cargo

An Officers' After
Duty Hours
Card Game.
An Army Chaplain
Came to the Game,
Probably to
Collect a Tithe for
the Chapel

44

Chapter 10
NCO School-President Kennedy

In April 1962, upon our return from LOTS, I was still assigned to
the S-3 office with Major Edward Dardis and 1/LT Bob Crowe. We were
busy writing reports on the LOTS and with regular training. Dardis
and Crowe gave me the responsibility of an NCO (Non-Commissioned
Officers) school with Sgt. Gonzalez as my assistant. The purpose of
the school was to determine candidates from the E-4 and E-3 ranks
that would fulfill leadership roles. Principles of Leadership were taught
as well as responsibilities of an NCO and their role in the Army. We
hoped to encourage re-enlistment as well as groom improved leaders.
The instructors managed to keep the attention of the pupils by having
interesting and practical sessions.

President John F. Kennedy came to New Orleans in May 1962, to
dedicate a wharf on the Mississippi River front. I was chosen to be the
officer in charge of the Army Platoon Honor Guard. Our platoon joined
the Honor Guard, commanded by a Coast Guard Admiral, with platoons
representing the Navy, Air Force, Marines, and Coast Guard. These
combined units were to honor the President as he landed at the civilian
New Orleans Airport, known now as the Louis Armstrong International
Airport. We were transported to the airport in a bus, wearing fatigues,
but carrying starched khakis, with white helmets, red scarves, and
white laces in our shined boots. We had weapons, but no ammunition.
The khaki pants had cans in the bottom of the pants to present a good
"blouse". We did look good. As we were about to leave CLJ, our
battalion photographer requested to go with us. I said OK, as long as he
had on his Class A uniform.

45

It was interesting to view the logistics and details of the President's visit. Cargo planes landed with the presidential limousine and other support vehicles. The presidential vehicle was driven on the tarmac to wait for the deplaning of the presidential party. Other planes landed in advance of Air Force One, with press members, security, and members of the President's staff. President Kennedy had the first presidential jet, a Boeing 707, as Air Force One. It landed and cruised to the appropriate spot. As it was taxiing to the unload spot, everyone came to attention and activity picked up.

The honor guard platoons were several yards from AF One, but we could view some of the welcoming party. JFK walked down the steps, followed by the Louisiana Congressional delegation. On the ground, he was met by Louisiana Governor Jimmy Davis and Mayor Victor Schiro, along with the New Orleans Police Escort. Our photographer was so excited to see the President in person that the first photo was out of focus; but he quickly recovered to make some outstanding black and white photos.

Off to the city the President went, riding in the presidential limousine with top down, joined by Gov. Davis and Mayor Schiro. As they departed, we were ordered to be "at ease", stack arms, and hang around. Having time on my hands, I decided to stroll over to AF One for a closer look. That stroll was cut short by the Secret Service, who wanted to know where I was going. "To look closer at AF One," I replied. The Secret Service officer said "No way," but I stated I was an Army officer, as he could clearly see, but no deal, so I hastily withdrew from the vicinity of the plane, being observed as I did.

As one could observe by looking at the tarmac as well as the roof of the airport terminal staffed with snipers with real weapons, there seemed to be plenty of security for the visit. The President returned approximately two hours later. We hoped he would "troop the line" of the military honor guard, but no luck. He did walk by and congratulate the escort from the New Orleans Police Department, and then returned to Air Force One for a quick departure. What a day…honor guard, viewing the president and related activities. A real memory maker.

Ed Hamilton, an associate of Uncle John F. Austin, Jr., requested a set of photographs of the day to be presented by him to Mayor Schiro. I learned that our photographer had turned his film over to the Navy, so I had to call the Navy station to receive the copies. I told them I was LT Austin. The rank of lieutenant in the Navy is equivalent to a captain in the Army, so the photos were quickly sent. Hamilton got his copy and gave the rest of the photos to the mayor.

Former New Orleans Mayor Shep Morrison was the Commanding General of a Transportation Division before he was appointed to be the ambassador to the Organization of Americas status by President Kennedy. Our units at CLJ had the duty to support the general and his troops at Grand Isle, LA, during their annual training. This must have been delayed in 1961 and 1962 due to

Air Force One brought President John F. Kennedy to New Orleans

the Berlin Crisis. There were many interesting and fun tales about the escapades at Grand Isle from the terminal troops at CLJ.

**An Army Honor Guard greeted
President Kennedy**

**A Marine Corps unit greeted the arrival of
Air Force One**

JFK in the presidential sedan touring
New Orleans

President Kennedy rode with Gov. Davis and
Mayor Schiro

49

Chapter 11
Lieutenants Protective Association
and Transfer

We lieutenants had a lot of idle time with nothing to do, so we started examining our situation of being extended. Our original active duty was for six months; then we were extended for another year. We soon realized that our individual release from active duty dates were one day shy of being promoted to First Lieutenants.

The promotion from 2nd Lieutenant to 1st Lieutenant was 18 months active duty, or three years from the date of commissioning. In jest, over drinks at the Officers Club, we started conversation of a "Lieutenants Protective Association" and how we could use the organization to gain our promotion. This was just a figure of speech to help pass the time. However, a draftsperson created a symbol for LPA…a snake wound around a gold bar and silver bar, proclaiming "LPA…Don't tread on me."

Several of us 2nd Lieutenants wrote letters to Congressmen, Senators, and other organizations. We later learned these letters were forwarded to Army brass, who in turn forwarded the letters to Camp Leroy Johnson. A few days later, I was told to meet with Lt. Col. Moorehead, our Battalion Commander. The first words out of his mouth: "What's with this Lieutenants Protective Organization?" A bit surprised that the LPO was subject of the meeting, quick thinking was needed; but the truth was better. I just told him this was a fantasy organization for all our conversation about being one day short of promotion. He was assured we were not officially organized, just having fun and laughs during our off-duty time. He emphasized that the Army did not encourage, nor did the Army tolerate any organized objection to Army Policy.

50

I'm not sure how, but Major Dardis was consulted and assured LTC Morehead that it was all in fun. We were told to discontinue the conversation on this subject at once...which we did. It had been fun. I did receive a letter from the Department of Army stating I would be welcome to re-enlist, thus receiving my promotion. The LPA disappeared just as fast as it started. I kept the emblem.

LTC Morehead, battalion commander, thought his troops would benefit from participating in the Toastmasters Club; so, we were urged to participate. There were a few weekly meetings, which were beneficial but were upstaged by the Berlin Crisis and other training requirements.

Later in the summer, I was transferred to the "Port", which was headquarters for the Transportation Terminal Command, known as 7500, which was located at the intersection of the Industrial Canal and Mississippi River (probably due to the LPA discussions.) The duty time there was boring with a capital "B". My first duty was to assist in creating an after-action report for the LOTS exercise on St. Joe Spit and just sit around. Get coffee, get lunch, and go home. I requested to return to CLJ where the action was, but was denied. At this time, I was living in an apartment with Charlie Martin and Pete Moffitt, enjoying life with them. I remained at 7500 until my separation date with the Army in September 1962. My last assignment was OIC of the CLJ softball team that participated in the Fourth Army softball tournament at Ft. Sill, Oklahoma. This was perfect timing for it allowed me to be in Texas when my son, Jeff Austin III was born on August 12, 1962. After his birth, I traveled to Ft. Sill, back to Texas and back to CLJ.

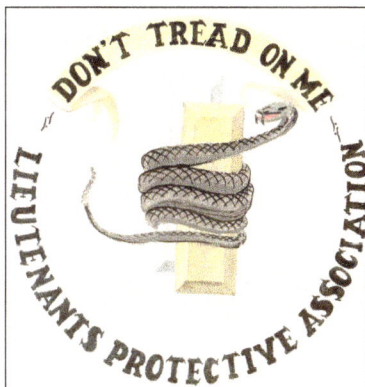

51

Chapter 12
People - Friends

It was my privilege to meet many capable, patriotic, loyal, humorous individuals who made quite an impression on me. I will share those memories and some of the "Rest of the Story" as Paul Harvey used to say (a popular ABC news commentator). As of January 2025, many years have passed since association with several of these men. The ROTC instructors at the University of Texas were Regular Army Officers whose rank had been reduced. These personnel had served in Korea, and possibly WWII. The military forces were reducing personnel and requiring college degrees for officers. Our ROTC Sergeant instructors were previously Majors, LT Colonels, or full bird Colonels. Due to their length of service, service record, and outstanding efficiency performances, they were downgraded to Master Sergeants (E-8) allowing them to reach retirement age and retire at the highest rank held during active duty.

Some of the officers at CLJ were under the same scrutiny, but on active duty as long time Captains. They had deadlines to be promoted or retire. Most had outstanding ratings for their performances, but were avid readers of the Army Times, which published a list of new promotions. These individuals had been in the Army, probably since their teens, and this is the only life they knew. Thus, they were striving for a promotion to Field Grade Officer (Major, then LT Colonel, and full Colonel) which would probably prolong their military career. Now, let's move on to a few of my memories:

Captain Edward P. Dardis (Major, Lt. Colonel)

Captain Dardis was my first Commanding Officer. He was a good mentor who made a great impact on me. He was an avid reader of the promotion lists, for he was 40 years old, had reviews or efficiency rating of "picket fences" (which was all ones). He was known for his knowledge, experience and efficiency. He made the list for Major and then when effective he was transferred to the Headquarters of the 394th Transportation Battalion as Operations Officer (S-3) ultimately to become the Battalion Executive Officer. He later had me transferred to his unit as an Assistant S-3.

As the situation in Vietnam continued to escalate, he was transferred to active units in that theater of war where he was instrumental in developing the use of the helicopter in combat and troop support. I understand he was promoted to LT Colonel during the conflict. I'm not sure if he was promoted to full Colonel. I received a letter from his wife, dated July 2, 2000. Captain Dardis had died from lung cancer after a battle of three- and one-half years. Dardis was a native of New Orleans and was kind enough to take a couple of us to a night out in his native ward in that city. It was like a "Street Car Named Desire" movie type of neighborhood. It was a real experience that can only occur with a native who will vouch for you. There were wooden buildings with windows opening to the sidewalk, with plenty of beer and snacks.

LT Colonel Thomas Morehead (Colonel)

He was the Commanding Officer of the 394th T BN (Term) during my duty at Camp Leroy Johnson in New Orleans. He was a good leader, he was fair, had a good military bearing, a good listener and recognized junior officers. I had to appear before LT Colonel Morehead for a misdirected prank. After the LOTS exercise, we junior officers had a lot of idle time. We thought it great that we had formed a "Lieutenants Protective Association" or LPA. We even had an emblem created by one of our draftsmen. The "club" had no agenda other than joking with drinks at the Officers Club. The fun soon ended when LT Colonel Morehead called me to his office to discuss this organization. The Army does not allow any organizing, but I had some difficulty explaining our fun to him. He was probably laughing at all of us, but Major Dardis vouched for us. The emblem disappeared and normal activity resumed. He retired from the US Army in 1974. During his career, he earned two Legions of Merit, a Purple Heart, two Bronze Stars, and the Combat Infantry Badge. He died in San Antonio on August 30, 2009, at age 91.

Jay and Betty Cummins

Jay was with me in the same Officer Basic Orientation Course at Fort Eustis. Jay was a graduate of North East Louisiana College, located in his home town of Monroe, Louisiana. He and wife Betty lived off post in Virginia and they were kind enough to invite me over a few times. Jay was good officer, laid back but effective.

The Cummins' lived in New Orleans in some apartments near the Gentilly Shopping center. Peter J's was a local bar where Jay, Jim Cox, and others, including myself, would often meet after duty and on weekends. There were lots of conversations. Betty and Jay were expecting their first child. Jay's cocktail buddies insisted if the child was a boy he should be named the Peter Jay Bar. Well, that did not go well with Betty. So...baby boy Scott Cummins (not Peter Jay Cummins) was born.

Jay and Betty offered me a ride home with them when the Officer Basic Course ended at Fort Eustis. We drove straight through to Monroe, LA, then to Shreveport where I was met by my father Jeff, Sr. We remained friends afterward and visits were exchanged. Sissy and I made a special trip to Monroe to get ideas on open boat houses. The Cummins drove us up and down the Ouachita River. We used these ideas as we built more piers and boat houses, of course setting the example and leading the way on Lake Jacksonville for this type of construction.

Betty and Jay lived on Gold Mine Plantation in Mangham, LA, after time in Alexandria and Shreveport, Louisiana, in the management of Scott Tractor dealerships. The Gold Mine Plantation, south of Monroe in the Ouachita River delta, produced cotton, soy beans, and later evolved to the cattle business. Sissy and I had a couple of visits to the plantation. Sissy thought slavery was still alive when she met June Bug, an employee of the Goldmine Plantation. My friend Jay died in 2022.

Charles Martin

Charlie was a graduate of Vanderbilt University, and was one Officers Basic class behind me. When assigned to the CLJ, he came to the 569th under Captain Dardis. As with most of us, he had several assignments within the battalion while on active duty. We became almost instant friends. Charlie lived off post in an apartment with Pete Moffitt. We remained friends after the Army; in fact, Charlie accompanied Sissy and me on our first date in 1970 to attend the Texas-OU game in Dallas. We only visited Nashville once, but corresponded fairly frequently. His wife is Brenda and they have three girls, all now married. One of the husbands is CEO of the Frost Arnett Company. The Martins, Moffitts, and Austins met in New Orleans around 2013 for a reunion of sorts. Camp Leroy Johnson was vacated and demolished years ago. A good time was had by all, even if we had a walking cane or two, and did not party as we would have during younger years. This was our last gathering. Charlie died in 2023.

Pete Moffitt

Pete was from High Point, North Carolina. He and Charlie attended the same Basic Class in Fort Eustis, and both came to the 394th for their first assignment. I lived with Pete and Charlie for a couple of months until my discharge. We still correspond. Jan is Pete's wife. He was a good officer. The Cuba Missile Crisis kept them busy. Pete was assigned as liaison to an Air Force Base.

Pete and Jan Moffitt

LT Pete Moffitt

First Lieutenant Robert E. (Bob) Crowe

Bob Crowe joined the 394th from an infantry assignment in Berlin. I worked with Bob in the S-3 office with Major Dardis. He was sort of intimidating until you knew him. We got to socialize with a group of young officers. We waterskied several times in Lake Pontchartrain. His goal was to become a dentist. Upon completion from his active duty, he returned to University of Mississippi to complete studies to gain admission to Dental School. As an undergraduate at Ole Miss, he was a member of Phi Delta Theta fraternity. He was another good mentor for me, and invaluable during the LOTS exercise in Florida. When in Berlin, he was on Check Point Charlie, the gate between East and West Berlin where the Russians had a large presence.

Bob joined the Mississippi National Guard as a Captain, was soon called to active duty during the unrest at the University of Mississippi campus in Oxford, MS. He relayed to me that he was more concerned with his own safety during the Oxford, Mississippi, riots than he was when facing the Russians in Berlin. A book, "An American Insurrection", describes the situation. We stayed in touch over the years. His dental practice was successful. He died around 2020.

Lt. Bob Crowe

57

The Grand Reunion of Army Buddies in New Orleans

Good Times in the French Quarter

Chapter 13
Texas National Guard and Personnel

I applied and was accepted to join the Texas Army National Guard in January 1963. My assignment was to the 49th Armored Division, Company B of the Second Battalion of the 144th Infantry. Company B was commanded by Captain Raben Jack Bolton. The company had units in both Jacksonville and Palestine, TX. I served in the 49th until separation on March 1, 1967. I quickly learned the Armored Infantry was quite different than a Transportation Corp Terminal Company.

When I first joined the Guard, we had weekly drills, which were changed a few months later to one weekend a month, with two weeks at North Fort Hood, Texas. Training was a difficult challenge for our unit while in Jacksonville or Palestine as there was no place to fire rifles or other weapons. We saw a lot of films and lectures, as well as drills. We had one Armored Personnel Carrier (APC), which had rubber treads to protect the city streets.

We were on duty the November 1963 weekend that President Kennedy was killed in Dallas, Texas. Governor Connally was also injured. We all wanted our unit dispatched to Dallas, but that was not to be. The 49th Division had been activated during the Berlin Crisis and stationed at Ft. Polk, Louisiana. Most of the soldiers stayed active with the unit, so military knowledge was good.

I did have one occurrence during my assignment to the Guard that caused me to re-think the length of service. Attendance at weekend Guard drills had not been good. We were ordered to send Sheriff Deputies to round up the absent guardsmen and bring them to meetings.

59

One guy was missing and could not be located on drill day. The Sheriff Deputy did locate him the following week at his place of work and took him to the sheriff's office.

The owner of the business, where the guardsmen worked, was highly inflamed at this arrest and made a straight line to the Austin Bank, where he proceeded to dress me up and down. Not many or any curse words, but he did not need them to get his point across. The boss stated his employee had a much more important assignment that day he missed the Guard meeting, which happened to be taking the boss's cattle to a show (now go figure). The guy who missed the meeting understood what I had to do, but he also had to follow his boss' instruction. There were no real hard feelings from the Guardsman as he remained a bank customer and acquaintance for years. These incidents, along with the military course requirements make me start to bring my National Guard days to a close.

I then transferred to Longview, TX to serve in the Headquarters Company. During weekends of Guard meetings, I would report to Longview, and then would visit the other Companies to observe their training. The other Battalion units were located in Rusk, Henderson, Atlanta, Kilgore, and Longview. I served in Longview until the Henderson unit had a problem with their full time sergeant. I was assigned to Henderson with Lt. Glenn Meadows to clean up the company until I left the Guard. The NCO in charge of Henderson had fake people on the payroll (a no-no). He was terminated. He was also known to take the unit's Tracked Personnel Carrier as his transportation to the Rio Palm Isle for Wednesday matinee.

The local National Guard armories could be used by the community for a small fee. This fee went into a local fund that could be used for the benefit of the Guard members. The community could use the building, but not for political reasons, as I found out the hard way. The Armory had been leased for our local Congressman to host a function. I later received a call from 49th Division Headquarters that I was in trouble because the building was used for political purposes. Thank goodness for some local friends who contacted General Harley B. West, then the commanding General of the 49th Armor Division. He was President of the Blue Cross-Blue Shield Insurance company in Dallas, so when a local major customer of Blue Cross called him, I was out of the "dog house". Lesson learned: NO POLITICAL ACTIVITIES IN A TEXAS ARMY NATIONAL GUARD ARMORY.

The members of the Palestine-Jacksonville unit were proficient at their military jobs as well as respected throughout the 144th Battalion, and it was a privilege and honor to serve with the following Guardsmen:

Captain Raben Jack Bolton
Because we are civilian-military members, military courtesy is strictly enforced during Guard activities. In non-military settings it was common to use names or titles. Jack Bolton was a native of Jacksonville. He served in Korea and probably in latter parts of WWII. I just assumed his commission was awarded on the Battlefield. He was a leader and all of us would willingly follow him into battle. As I recall he wore the Infantry Combat Badge. He was well respected, and Company B reacted to his orders and thoughts. We all knew he had been there and done that. Jack lived in Palestine; he and his wife had two children. I'm not sure when he joined or retired from the Guard, but his service probably provided some retirement for him.

61

Captain James Hinsley

Jim was employed by the Texas Department of Public Safety and was a long time Army Guard Captain. I'm not sure of his wartime service, but he was with the Company when it was activated in 1961. He was a good man. As a Highway Patrolman, he was working a traffic stop, standing between the two cars, when a vehicle crashed into his patrol car and pushed Jim into the car in front. He had severe injuries, but he did recover to return to duty with the Highway Patrol. I liked Jim, but at times his military bearing was not good, and he did not take responsibility.

As we returned to the Jacksonville Armory after two weeks at Ft. Hood, he told us if it were up to him, we could be dismissed. But Captain Bolton had instructed him to be sure all our equipment was cleaned before anyone was dismissed. There was no problem with cleaning equipment, for it was standard practice to do so, but for him to blame it on Captain Bolton was wrong. He remained in the Guard past officer retirement age, but his rank was reduced to Sergeant in order to allow him to be in the Guard.

First Sergeant Jeter Cook

Sgt. Cook was a full time employee of the Texas National Guard. We never had any problem with required records or payroll. A quiet person, but you never wanted to be on his bad side. He knew the rules, regulations, and how to handle his role as First Sergeant very well. His personal life was likewise a model for others.

62

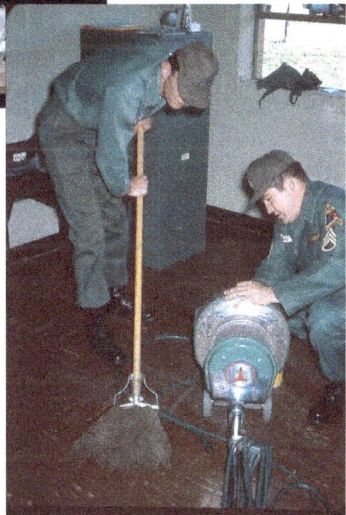

**Activities at the Jacksonville
National Guard Armory**

Chapter 14
Take-Aways from Army Experiences

These are my takeaways from my active duty and National Guard service. My active and Texas National Guard service time was in a period of relative peace for the U.S. The conflict in Vietnam had not escalated, but we did experience a buildup due to the Berlin Crisis. The Russians built the Berlin Wall to separate communist held countries from the western allied countries.

The Cuban Missile Crisis was building as I was leaving the Army. I had noticed a buildup of material, vehicles, etc., at the port area.

The Vietnam war escalated after I joined the 49th Armored Division of the Texas National Guard. We were never mentioned or prepared for a "call up". One could watch the war on television at night. The 49th did have an increase in enlistments from guys avoiding tour of duty in Vietnam.

The time spent on active duty was an opportunity to be yourself after college. Living in New Orleans, in the Army, I was on my own. It was a time to grow up, and take responsibility for men, equipment and my actions. The veteran officers and non-coms had plenty of patience with young, green officers. One just had to listen to them.

These years were learning years: learning to respect a chain of command, learning to communicate, learning to be responsible for people in your command, learning to plan, learning to teach classes, learning to respect people, learning to discipline people fairly, and mostly learning to learn. Most of all it was learning to be an adult and being responsible for your actions, in the military and personally.

This memoir was begun in 1962, written in pencil. It surfaced again in 2024 as I was reviewing old files. It was fun reviewing what transpired in the earlier years of my life and to relive those times. History and time have allowed me to edit and explain a bit more, but it all happened, and that's my story. Who will read this? I'm not sure, but I hope you will enjoy it.

Jeff and Sissy Austin

www.ingramcontent.com/pod-product-compliance
Lightning Source LLC
Chambersburg PA
CBHW042338040426
42447CB00018B/3478